Role Performance of Continuing Education Workers

Role Performance of Continuing Education Workers

Role Performance of Continuing Education Workers

G. Lokanadha Reddy
&
A. Kusuma

DISCOVERY PUBLISHING HOUSE
NEW DELHI—110 002

First Published—2000
Reprinted: 2013

ISBN 81-7141-

Published by :
Discovery Publishing House
4831/24, Ansari Road, Prahlad Street
Darya Ganj, New Delhi—110 002 (INDIA)
Phone : 3279245
Fax.: 91-11-3253475

Laser Typeset by :
Allied Computers
Karnal (Haryana)

Printed at :
Dynamic printers, Delhi

Foreword

Research studies in the area of Teachers Role performance have been conducted at school level from as early as 1950 in India. Such an emphasis has not been given to the studies related to adult education teachers role performance. It is only for the last two decades a few studies have been undertaken to examine the various aspects of organization of the Adult Education programmes in this country. The studies conducted on adult education instructors role performance are limited in number. Here, it is to be highlighted that teaching children is fairly different from adults especially in developing functional literacy skills. Adult education is concerned with science of teaching adults. It is of recent origin and very little work has been done in this country to examine this concept and its applications in teaching of adults. The study undertaken by Dr. G. Lokanadha Reddy, and Dr. A. Kusuma is of great significance in this content.

The authors made an attempt to examine the influence of Socio-Psychological variables affecting the role performance of adult continuing education workers. They has taken fairly large sample of adult/continuing education workers neo literates and community representatives. They studied the influence of the adult/continuing education workers characteristics such as sex, age, educational status, community background, attitude, personality on their role performance. I am confident that the findings of the study are of great relevance to the adult education functionaries organizing inservice and pre-service training programmes. I am sure that this book which includes the conceptual discussion about the adult education workers multi-dimensional roles and performance of such roles by the continuing education workers will be of great help to all concerned in adult/continuing education programmes of this country.

The target readers of this book would include the field practitioners and researchers of adult education apart from students of this area which is gradually emerging as a specialized field of study in education. I have no hesitation to say that all the above mentioned target groups will find this book very useful.

Dr. S. Mohan
Professor and Head
Department of Education
Alagappa University
Karaikudi—623 003

Preface

While adding this book to the list of books already adorning the galaxy of adult education, the authors do not feel apologetic for the same because that this book had its own unique features by way of its mode of approach to the various intricate variables invariably involved in the role performance of adult continuing education workers. It is our earnest attempt to expound the essentials of the subject matter as a result of our own study and experiences in adult continuing education.

In adult education, the post literacy worker/continuing education worker is the key figure and the success of the programme largely depends on his/her performance. As a frontline worker, he has to perform different activities in different marked situations. Broadly speaking, he has to perform the roles such as teaching, organization and community roles. Several personal and psychological factors may contribute in performing their roles effectively. The present book is aimed to identify certai socio-psychological factors affecting the role performances of adult continuing education workers. The role performance of adult continuing education workers is rated by 100 adult continuing education workers (self-rating), 200 neo-literates (neo-literate rating) and 100 community representatives (community ratings). The investigators have also studied the influence of adult continuing education workers characteristics such as age, sex, educational status community, attitude towards adult education and personality characteristics on their role performance.

The book is presented in six chapters. In chapter 1, brief introduction of the topic is given. Chapter 2 deals with the review of related literature on the concept role performance of teachers. The Chapter 3 deals with statement of the problem and the 4th one describes the research tools selected, developed and used for the study, the sample frame, data collection and statistical techniques used. The Chapter 5th contians data analysis, testing of hypotheses and presentation and interpretation of findings. The last one forms the summary and conclusions.

It is just fitness of things to state here that this book is prepared to meet the requirements of adult continuing education teachers, teacher trainers and research scholars working in the field of adult education. We do not know to what extent we have succeeded in our attempt but we will feel amply rewarded if this book can further the understanding of the concept role performance of adult continuing education workers. Any constructive suggestion for the betterment of this work will be greatly acknowledged.

Authors

Contents

1

Introduction

Introduction

Education plays a vital role in developing human resources in any country. It is a means for qualifying human resources to utilize the physical resources fully and effectively promoting knowledge, understanding, attitude and skill. Realizing the importance of education in the socio-economic development of the individual and the country as a whole, the Government of India has made several efforts for the promotion of literacy among the masses by launching a number of adult education programmes. The National Adult Education Programme was launched on 2nd October, 1978, throughout the country to make 100 million illiterate adults into literate. The progress of the programme was reviewed by evaluating the same periodically. In the light of the findings of the evaluation reports, the programme was further strengthened by launching the National Literacy Mission (NLM) to cover 80 million illiterates in the country by 1995.

The experience in the field of adult education shows that in the absence of learning environment and effective programme of post-literacy and continuing education, the efforts made in literacy programmes yielded extremely limited results. The NLM has rightly stressed the importance of post-literacy and continuing education. Consequently, the Government of India in Feb. 1988, decided to establish Jana Shikshan Nilayams (JSN) with an intention to institutionalize the post-literacy and continuing education to create facilities, to enable the learners to continue their learning beyond elementary level and to create scope for the application of their learning for improvement of their living condition. Each JSN will cover a cluster of 4–5 villages with a population of about 5,000 and is manned by a worker known as "Prerak or Post Literacy Worker". With the advent of Total Literacy Programmes launched in several districts in recent years, the concept of post-literacy programmes also gained momentum in several states of India. As a result, post literacy volunteers/workers have been appointed and these workers are taking care of the post literacy activities in their respective communities.

Importance of the Teacher in Adult Education Programme

The success of the post literacy programmes largely depends on the performance of the post literacy workers. As it is well aware that there are various things involved in an educational programme. Any educational programme has four components—the learner, the teacher, the content and the method. This is more true in case of adult/continuing education. The success of adult/continuing education programme depends on a number of factors, out of which the literacy worker is a key figure. As a frontline worker in the Adult Education Programme, he is responsible for teaching-learning activities directing the experience of adults towards well defined ends. He/She is the actual "doer" of adult education in the community. He is the organiser of the literacy centre, teacher of literacy, generator of awareness, helps in economic development, mobilizer of community resources for the benefit of the learners and recorder of the process of change and learning. The Report of the Review Committee on the National Adult Education Programme (1981) emphasized that the "The Programme of Adult Education vitally depends on the initiative and on the skill of the instructor/teacher. The improved physical facilities, teaching techniques, suitable teaching learning materials supplement the adult education teachers efficiency but, they are not the substitute for an effective teacher/post literacy worker. The importance of an effective post literacy worker for the successful implementation of adult/continuing education programme is undisputable.

Role and Functions of the Post Literacy Worker/Prerak/Instructor

The Adult Education workers are called 'Instructors', 'Social Educators', 'Animators', 'Organisers', 'Post Literacy Workers', and sometimes 'Teachers'. Whatever may be the title, they are the key figure in the adult education programme. As a front line worker, he has to perform several roles and the success of the programme largely depends on his role performance. As already stated that the adult education teachers are responsible for building awareness among the learners about their situation in the society, the difficulties they face and the possibilities to improve their livers. They are also expected to organise themselves about their rights and duties. They are also expected to organise skill development programmes to the learners to increase their skills, gain more knowledge about the present occupation or future occupation. It is also inevitable for the instructors to strengthen the literacy skills already acquired by the neo-literates and made them to use these literacy skills in day to day life. To do all these activities, the instructor should update and upgrade his professional knowledge from time to time by attending seminars, workshops and meetings related to adult education. It is needless to say that community participation and support are inevitable for the success of any community development. In adult education programme also, community participation and involvement leads the creation and maintenance of proper learning environment. This involves the post literacy worker to create and sustain adequate interest among the learners and utilize the local institutional and community resources both human and material resources for effective functioning of adult education programme. In order to perform the above activities, the adult education teacher has to perform several broader roles such as teaching roles, organisational roles and community roles. The performance of the post literacy worker largely depends on the capacity of overcoming the social problems, his attitude towards adult education, his social participation etc. The evaluation of NAEP at Central and State levels by different agencies reveal that the success of the programme depends not only on curriculum, method of teaching, teaching learning materials but also the post literacy worker and his social and psychological factors.

Need for the Study

Research in the field of the adult education has been scanty in India because educationists till recently have concentrated more on pedagogical than anragogical research. What is needed at the present crucial stage of the programme is that there is a paucity of reference materials identifying the characteristics associated with the role performance of adult/continuing education teachers, and an effort in this direction is needed.

Researches in adult education have not paid sufficient attention to identify the socio-psychological factors affecting the role performance of adult education teachers working in the post Literacy programmes and are considered as one of the important areas. Moreover, factors such as teachers age, sex, educational qualification and community are also contributing to their role performance. As it has already been reported that a person with positive attitude towards adult education and commitment to his work can do his work effectively. The role performance depends on number of factors like attitude, personality, level of education and community background etc. The present study is aimed at analysing the role performance of adult/continuing education worker in relation to the selected characteristics of him/her. To identify the necessary conditions conducive for the role performance of adult/continuing education worker and the prerequisite personality characteristics for an effective post literacy worker will be highly useful for Programme trainers and organisers. Researchers like Malakondaiah (1980), Reddy, P.A. (1984), Reddeppa. G. (1993) identified the characteristics and qualities of successful instructors. Mathur (1975) identified some of the characteristics of teachers as liked by the illiterate adults. Similarly, Manuswamy (1980), Nath, J.C. (1981) measured instructors attitude towards NAEP. Likewise, Reddy, G. L. (1985), Muthuchamy (1991) studied the role performance of adult education instructors in Indian context.

Considerable attempts have been made in abroad to identify the competencies required by an adult educator. Chamberline (1961), Malcoln, Knowles (1972), and Vevi (1968), Sungkahand (1981), Sominar (1975) have identified the performance requirements of adult education teachers. The researches clearly indicate that no systematic attempt has been made by the researchers in India to identify the role performance of adult/continuing education teachers and the psycho-social factors associating with their role performance. The present study is an attempt to identify the role performance of adult/continuing education teachers and the socio-psychological factors associated with their role performance.

The detailed review of related literature is presented in the succeeding chapter.

2

Review of Related Literature

Introduction

The efficiency of the adult education programme is primarily determined by the efficiency of adult/continuing education teacher. The adult/continuing education teacher role performance is influenced by several factors such as his personality, attitude towards the programme and the variables such as age, sex, educational qualification and community background of the teacher. Hence, knowledge of the factors that contribute to the performance of the teacher in discharging his roles is essential both for the recruitment of effective teachers and for promoting efficiency among them. Such knowledge can be acquired only through empirical research of the area. Research studies conducted both in India and abroad in the field of adult education shows that not much attention has been paid by the researchers to study and explain precisely the nature of adult/continuing education teacher role performance.

An overview of the research studies already done in the area will be of an immense use to the researchers in giving direction for their further research. It also helps in identifying the factors that are related to adult education teachers role performance. With this background, the review of related literature is presented in the following pages under the headings namely :

— Studies on qualities and characteristics of adult education teachers.

— Studies on competencies possessed by adult education teachers.

— Studies on factors related to instructors/adult education teachers effectiveness.

— Studies on determinants of adult education teachers effectiveness and role performance.

— Studies on teacher role expectations.

Studies on Qualities and Characteristics of Adult Education Teachers

Reddy and Kumaraswamy (1984) identified the following characteristics of an effective adult education instructor : uses a variety of teaching methods, uses humour, organise the adult education centre effectively and encourage learners to work hard. Adinarayana Reddy and Chalapathi Reddy (1985) also identified similar characteristics of an effective adult education instructor in a different study.

Cass (1971) through his study found that a successful teacher of adults establishes personal relationship with each individual, builds his instruction around the needs and goals of the individuals, selected methods and techniques which are appropriate to the situation, creates a suitable learning atmosphere, teaches students the skills they need in their daily activities and provides them with suitable learning experience.

Cobley (1976) also identified almost similar qualities among effective adult education instructors namely : fairness and sense of humour, desire to acquire more knowledge, good speaking and communicating ability, concern towards students interest and individual differences, interest in the use of various methods of teaching and in stimulating discussion.

Knox (1971) review of twenty studies on adult education teachers came to the conclusion that a gap is always found between average and outstanding teaching. According to him, the difference will be found in experience, knowledge of subject matter, familiarity with teaching methods, time spent on preparation and in his/her personality to get along with adult students.

Malakondaiah (1980) identified the characteristics of an effective adult education instructor viz., mutual cooperation with learners, capacity to organise the adult education programme successfully, knowledge of the subject, good eloquence, honesty, respect for moral values and ability to understand adult learners.

A knowledge of more than one area, ability to deal with abstract content, experience to work with unskilled people and ability to establish social contacts are considered by the National Association for Public School Adult Education (1986) as attributes of the successful adult educators.

Pearce (1960) lists the characteristics of effective instructors of adults based on the opinions collected by him from a sample of students, teachers and administrators. This list covers characteristics like flexibility, patience, practicability, creativity and ability to develop and maintain self-confidence of adult learners to reach the goal.

The study of Rogers (1969) has identified certain ideal qualities of adult education instructors. They are :

a) fair dealings
b) sense of Humour
c) fondness of knowledge
d) ability to speak and communicate well
e) liking for people informal
f) a good organizer uses lesson plans
g) counsels students
h) a good listener
i) an enthusiastic teacher
j) use of various methods of teaching
k) a careful observant
l) knows student's interest
m) has neat appearance
n) uses visual aids
o) stimulates discussion
p) raises questions
q) knows sources of information
r) considers individual differences
s) relates well to students
t) suggests further study
u) confidence in students
v) well prepared
w) motivates learning and
x) maintain interests in subjects.

According to Tripathi (1977) the characteristics of successful instructors in non-formal education programmes are; ability to establish rapport with learners, respect for adult learners, ability to draw a curriculum to meet the environment needs of the learners, flexibility in exhibition of leadership qualities.

Yesanna's (1986) survey shows that factors like communication skills, interest in teaching, co-operativeness and friendliness, knowledge in the subject matter, moral values and learners activities are related to instructor effectiveness.

From the description of the findings of the above studies, it appears that the terms, qualities, characteristics and attributes are used to describe more or less the same type of factors associated with effectiveness of adult education instructors.

Studies on Competencies Possessed by the Adult Education Teachers

Aker (1962) based on his study listed 23 types of behaviour patterns which are considered as adequate competencies for determining the achievement of educational objectives by instructors. They are as given below :

— helps people to control and adjust to change rather than maintain the status quo.

— intelligently observes and listens to what is being said or done and uses this information guiding his respondents.

— selects and uses teaching method, materials and resources that are appropriate in terms of what is to be learned and in terms of the needs and abilities of the individual learner.

— helps his client to acquire the ability for critical thinking.

— provides an atmosphere where adults are free to search through trial-and-error without fear of instructional or interpersonal threat.

— identifies potential leaders and helps them to develop their potentials and capacities.

— make use of existing values, beliefs, customs and attitudes as a starting point for educational objectives.

— is actively involved in continuing study that will increase his professional competence.

— understands the role of adult education in society and is aware of the factors and forces that give rise to this function.

— actively shares, participates and learns with the learners in learning experience.

— helps adults to actively set their goals and provides a variety of means and opportunities for intensive self-evaluation.

— identifies and interprets trends that have implications for adult education.

— has clearly defined his unique role as an adult educator and understands his responsibility for performing it.

— arranges learning experiences so that learners can integrate theory and practice.

— is effective in building a teaching team among lay leaders and group members.

— uses the process of appraisal to evaluate programmes and to help clarify and change objectives.

— is creative and imaginative in developing new programmes and experiments that are necessary for the expansion of adult education.

— make use of the contributions of all group members through the utilization of individual talents and abilities.

— works with schools, teachers, parents and pre-adults so as to assist them in developing motivation, attitudes, understanding and skills necessary for life-long learning.

— objectively presents contrasting points of view.

— assumes the initiatives in developing a strong rational perception of importance and essentiality of continuing education.

— recognises when the communication process is not functioning adequately or when it breaks down.

— identifies, critically evaluates and discusses scholarly works by investigators in adult education and related fields.

Grabowski (1976) identified ten competencies necessary for effective adult educators. They are as described below :

— understands and takes into account the motivational and participation patterns of adult learners.

— understands and provides for the needs of adults in learning.

— well-versed in the theory and experiences in the practice of adult education.

— knows the community and its needs.

— knows how to use the various methods and techniques of instruction.

— possess communication skills, including listening.

— has an open mind and provides an atmosphere that allow adults to pursue their needs and interests.

— continues his own education.

— is able to appraise and evaluate programmes.

Competencies like basic understanding about programme organisation and administration, ability to establish wholesome relationships and executive and supervisory ability occupy high priority in the study made by Mandry (1963).

Mocker (1974) identified 291 behaviours, attitudes and knowledge which should be exhibited by a competent adult basic education teacher.

Pandiyammal (1989) conducted a study on competencies needed for adult education animators. The study reveals that the animators of the sample appear to be competent in not of the competencies/ statements identified various roles assigned to them. Further, it is noted that animators with better educational qualifications, animators belonged to schedule castes and woman animators are more competent than the animators with less qualifications, animators with other cases and men animators respectively.

According to White (1950) competencies appropriate for adult educators are as given below :

— to gain a better understanding of the basic needs which causes adults to participate in educational programmes.

— to gain a clear insight into the changing interests of adults in vocations, religion, family, leisure time activities, health and other areas of life.

— to increase ability to apply psychological principles to the selection of objectives.

— to acquire techniques for relating the programme more closely to the needs and the interests of adults.

- to acquire techniques for relating the Programme more closely to the general needs of the community.
- to become more skillful in recognising community needs and resources that are important to adult education programmes.
- to develop a better understanding of the kinds of educational methods most suitable for mature persons.
- to become familiar with procedures for keeping up with new developments and materials for adult education programme.

Competencies listed under various studies described above appear to be by and large functions or roles expected to be performed as effective instructors of adults.

Studies on Factors related to Instructor/Adult Education Teacher Effectiveness

Reddy (1985) identified that instructor effectiveness is closely related to sex, age, educational qualifications and occupation of the instructor. The results also confirmed that female instructors and instructors with higher education qualifications are found to be effective.

Reddy (1989) formulated a study to identify the factors associated with instructors effectiveness with the following objectives :

- to examine whether men and women instructors differ significantly in their effectiveness.
- to study the difference in the effectiveness of younger (25 years and below) and older instructors (25 years and above).
- to know whether instructors having low education (VII and IX Class level) differ from instructors with high education level (X Class and above).
- to understand the role of achievement motivation in instructor effectiveness.
- to know how far exposure to mass media influences the effectiveness of instructors.
- to examine how far the attitude towards adult education effects the effectiveness of instructors.
- to explore the role of various personality characteristics on instructor effectiveness and

— finally, to estimate the amount of influence exerted by various independent variables closer a instructor effectiveness.

The following conclusions were drawn from the results of the investigation :

— Women can function more effectively than men and instructors of adults as per learners and cumulative rating.

— The age of instructors did not come in the way of the discharge of his duties as instructor effectively.

— Higher the achievement motive possessed by an instructor to more effective will he be as an instructor.

— Improvement in the educational status of an instructor with high achievement motive seems to improve his effectiveness's an instructor of adults.

— Older instructors with high positive attitude towards adult education were more effective as instructors than younger instructors with high positive attitude (as per learners and cumulative rating).

— By and large instructors with high positive attitude towards adult education seem to be more successful in their profession than instructors with low positive attitude towards adult education.

— Women instructors with high exposure to mass media seem to be more effective than men instructors with high exposure to mass media.

— In general, instructors will exposed to mass media appear to have an edge over instructors with low exposure to mass media in their effectiveness as instructor.

— Effective adult education instructors seems to possess majority of the traits exhibited by high scorers on factors A, B, C, D, E, F, G, H, Q and Q_2 (as measured by Cahell's 16 Personality Factor Questionnaire).

— Majority of the qualities attributed a low scores on factors I, L, M, O and Q_4 also appear desirable for effective adult instructors.

— Regression analysis (taking measure of instructor effectiveness) based on community rating indicated variable, education, factor–Q_2, Q_3 E and F as significantly influencing effectiveness of instructors and they together accounted 21.9 percent of variance.

— Regression analysis (taking measure of instructor effectiveness) based on learners rating indicates variables, Factor-O, sex, mass media, Exposure, Achievement Motivation, Education, Factor M, F, C and A as significantly influencing effectiveness of instructors and they together accounted 18.14 per cent of variance.

— Regression analysis (taking measure of instructors effectiveness) based on cumulative rating indicated variables, factor Q, sex, Factor E, F mass media exposure and Achievement motivation as significantly influencing effectiveness of instructors and they together accounted 8.63 per cent of variance.

Bhandari and Mehta (1974), through their study, found that persistency and dropout of adult learners in the literacy centres largely depends on the background, abilities and aptitudes of instructors. They have also found significant relationship between educational qualification and performance.

Murad (1971) experimenting with various types of literacy teachers in order to draw a generalised profit of literacy teachers representing agricultural milieu, stated that the literacy teacher should complete 20 years of age and should belong to the same milieu as his students.

Based on his study Shrivastava (1981) state that young educated farmer is a good choke for agriculture oriented literacy.

Vijayalakshmi (1985) studied the attitude and opinion of adult education instructors towards their profession. Her study indicated that positive attitude possessed by instructors has significant positive impact on their effectiveness as instructors.

Upadhyay (1986) identified the factors related to the performance of the instructors and suggested the suitable models for selection of adult education instructors. The findings indicate that females, aged between 20–30 years with primary education with more sources of income, local and those associated with more political parties proved to be as highly performed instructors.

The above studies clearly indicate only very few studies have been conducted systematically to find out the variables or characteristics that are associated with instructor effectiveness. Hence, there is every need to take up systematic investigations to delineate the variables that are closely associated with the instructor effectiveness.

Studies on Determinants of Adult Education Teacher Effectiveness and Role Performance

Alkana and Henriques (1982) reported that majority of the instructors covered by their survey participated in the adult Programme of pupil motives like involving themselves in the education development of the area, to supplement their income to gain teaching experience and to oblige the request/order from certain persons, whom they respected.

According to the Report of Work Oriented Adult Literacy Pilot Project (1973), instructors motives for participating in adult literacy projects were—patriotism, personal interest, increase in income, desire to contribute to progress, circumstances change in occupations and the like.

Ankaiah (1982) identified that the instructor interests in participating in adult education programme are related to personal, social, political, moral, teaching, economic and cultural factors.

Chaterjee (1969) reported four types of motives expressed by voluntary teachers enrolled in the adult literacy programme. They are: to learn the art of teaching adults, to learn about agriculture and other new things, to have an opportunity to serve villagers and to earn extra money.

Among the instructors representing Hariharan and Rao (1982) study, a good number (48 per cent) of instructors stated social service as the main motive in working for adult education. Another group (40 per cent) expressed the motive of making villagers literate few instructors wanted to create social awareness. Some wanted to utilize the time available with them and others joined as instructors due to unemployment.

Janardhana Naidu (1980) measured the attitude of adult education instructors towards various aspects of NAEP and found majority of the instructors possessed positive attitude towards adult education programme.

Krishna Reddy (1981) enquired into the job satisfaction of NAEP instructors and identified their job dissatisfaction. The factors are—insecurity of job, low salary, lack of rural libraries, lack of adequate teaching-learning materials and aids.

Reddy (1985) in his study "Role Performance : Discrepancy between Ideology and Practice" observed the discrepancy in the instructors' roles as 'Organizer of cultural and Recreational Programmes', 'Teacher of Literacy and Disseminator of Functional Information 'mobilizer of Resources' and 'Guidance Activities'.

Madana Mohan Reddy (1985) identified the performance requirements of an adult education instructor. Mallikarjuna (1987) identified the determinants of effective communication in adult education centre as perceived by the instructor's.

Reddy (1992) conducted a study on the determinants of Adult Education Instructor Effectiveness. The following are drawn from the results of the Investigation :

— Women were rated as more effective instructors than man instructors.

— Younger instructors were proved to be effective than older instructors.

— Cast did not come in the way of discharging the duties of the instructors.

— It appears that there is no influence of level of education on instructor effectiveness.

— Unmarried instructors belonging to other than coolies and agriculturists were rated as more effective instructors.

— Instructors belonging to other than coolies and agriculturists were rated as more effective instructors.

— Size of land holding and instructor effectiveness and not related to each other.

— Income of the instructors does not relate to the instructor effectiveness.

— Cinema seeing behaviour of the instructors was affecting their effectiveness.

— Newspaper reading habit of instructors enhances their effectiveness.

— Exposure of mass media agencies will increase the effectiveness of the instructors.

— Laser the urban pull more will be the effectiveness of the instructor.

— Higher the achievement motivation possessed by the instructors and higher will be effectiveness.

— Instructors with high positive attitude were proved to be more effective as instructors.

— Effective adult education instructors seem to possess majority of the traits exhibited by low scores on factor C, E, Q_1 and Q_4 on the other hand, qualities attributed to top scores on factor G and M were also appear to be desirable for effective adult education instructor.

— Regression analysis of the instructor effectiveness based on learners rating indicated the variables—newspaper, attitude, television, radio, mass media exposure, land, age, cinema, occupation, Factor C and Factor E as significantly influencing effectiveness of instructors and they together accounted 20.45 per cent of variance.

— Regression analysis of the instructor effectiveness based on self-rating of the instructors showed cinema, occupation, radio, television, mass media exposure, land holdings urban pall, factor Q_2, Factor C and Factor M has significantly influencing the effectiveness of instructors and they put together accounted about 48.06 per cent of variance.

— Regression analysis of instructor effectiveness based on cumulative rating indicated variables factor M, achievement motivation, urban pal, television, Factor Q_4, A_3, Cinema, attitude, ratio and factor Q_2 as significantly influencing the effectiveness of instructors and they put together accounted about 9.17 per cent of variance.

Reddeppa (1993) studied the determinants of Prerak effectiveness. The findings reveals the following :

— The Preraks selected for organisation of JSNS are men, unprivilege section belongs to agricultural background from lower income groups, with less education, less experienced, married and belong to younger in age.

— As per all sources of rating viz., learners, community and cumulative are majority of the selected sample belongs to effective group.

— Association between prerak characteristics and effectiveness reveals that the association between and effectiveness is significant from all sources of rating. Further, sex and effectiveness is also significantly associated as per learners ratings point of view.

— There is no significant difference between men and women Preraks in their effectiveness. However, the effectiveness scores that women

Preraks were found to be more effective.

— Preraks belongs to forward caste were found to be more effective followed by the group.

— Preraks with agricultural background were found to be more effective than income groups.

— Preraks with more experience in betrays works were found to be more effective.

— Preraks with more education were found to be more effective workers.

— Married preraks were found to be more effective than unmarried preraks.

— Preraks in the higher age groups were found to be more effective than younger preraks.

— Preraks with more positive attitude were found to be more effective than those with less positive attitude.

On the other hand, Subhashini (1985) delineated obstacles for effective communication process in adult education centres as perceived by the instructor.

Studies on Teacher Role Expectations

Bledsoe and Brown (1968) conducted a study on "Role perception of Secondary School Teachers as related to people perceptions of teacher behavioural characteristics". In this, the role expectations of 178 Georgia Secondary teachers were measured by TPQ (Teacher Practice Questionnaire), pupils perceptions was measured by Pupil Observation Survey (POS) and pupils attitudes were analysed by sex, age, experience, perception, field grade level and selected interaction efforts.

The results drawn from the study were Science and Mathematics teachers perceived the advice information given role more important than the social studies teachers. Age and sex differentially influenced the teachers perceptions of the motivator role. For the disciplinarian role, grade level and the interaction effect of sex by field were significant.

Soles (1964) conducted a study on "Teacher Role Expectations and the Internal Organisation of Secondary Schools". The basic idea of the study was that some of the sources of role-expectations or pressure and demands upon individual personnel (teachers) in the small work unit (class-room) may be rooted in the particular type of structural arrangement of the organisation (school). In this study teacher role expectations were regarded as dependent variable within the organisational structure of the school.

Sorenson, Husex and Constance Yu (1963) through their study developed an instrument designed to assess teacher role expectations. A preliminary form administered to 284 students was designed to measure 6 role dimensions namely—information given, disciplinarian, adviser counselor, motivator and referer. A factor analysis confirmed these 6 factors and provided as basis for a revised form which was administered to 94 students. The results also were factor analysed. On the basis of the 2 studies a revised set of key was developed for 5 of the 6 scales.

Adviser and information given scales were combined to form a single scale. Reliability estimates for the scale range from .77 to .93. The scales have low to moderate inter-correlation.

To measure of teacher role expectation, the tool used were an adaptation of the Valenti-Nelson (1951) Survey of teaching practices which consists of the 012 paired comparison statements dealing with a variety of situations which teacher encounter in the teaching role. Built into the instrument were 17 different issues such as : handling minor disciplinary problems, dealing with individual differences, planning class-room work, motivating pupils, dealing with student organisations. There are alternative methods of handling each of these issues. Each alternative is consistent with one of the four models. Role–A impersonal, Role-B self sufficient, Role-C counseling and Role-D Group development.

The results of the study indicated firstly that the teachers from multiple period type schools did emphasize the group development role-expectations. Secondly, teachers in the single-period curriculum scheduling schools did have significantly higher mean staff scores on the technical self-sufficient direction. Thirdly, no significant differences were found between staff role-scores from the multiple and single period type schools for either the impersonal bureaucratic (Role-A) or the counseling and guidance (Role-C).

An Overview of the Research Reviewed

An overview of the research reviewed clearly reveals that a good number of studies have been conducted on Adult Education Teacher Effectiveness, Characteristics of Effective Teachers, Competencies required by the adult education teachers, determinants of adult education teacher effectiveness both in India and abroad. Further, a few studies have been noted with regard to the determinants of adult education teacher effectiveness and role performance apart from studies on teacher role expectations in the formal system of education. But, when we analyse the studies, the Research on role performance of post literacy/ continuing education workers, the output is still inadequate for a greater understanding of the phenomena. Specific studies examining the role-performance of post-literacy/continuing education workers are more warranted. Further, studies which probe into the role performance of post literacy workers in relation to the age, sex, community, educational qualifications are more needed for deeper understanding of the concept. Attempts are also needed to study the influence of psychological factors related to the role performance of continuing education workers and the present study is an attempt in this direction. The statement of the problem is presented in the succeeding chapter.

3

Statement of the Problem

Introduction

The review of literature presented in Chapter 3 clearly shows that no comprehensive attempts have been made to identify the role performance of post literacy/continuing education workers, in relation to their socio, psychological factors.

Statement of the Problem

'A Study of Certain Socio-Psychological Factors Affecting the Role Performance of Adult/Continuing Education Workers'.

Meaning of the Terms Used in the Study

The operational definitions of the terms used in the study :

Role : Role means actor's part in a play/what one is appointed to carryout the activities or a role can be designed as a bundle of expectations. It is possible that an individual can play many roles. The later make different demands on the individual, thus bringing about a situation of intra-role conflict, furthermore, sociologists use the concept role-seat for the who is collection of roles which are played by an individual.

Performance : The mode of performance is the process of internalizing an idea or using a practice habitually, so that, it becomes a fundamental part of the way in which a person thinks about an undertakes his or her work.

Adult/Continuing Education Worker : The Adult Continuing Education worker is a person incharge of organising post literacy and continuing education programmes in the National Adult Education Programme.

Socio-psychological Factors : In this study, the factors considered are sex, age, educational qualification and the community of the instructor and attitude of post-literacy worker/continuing education worker, and personality of the worker.

In this study, the role performance of post literacy workers refers to perform their roles as teaching activities, organisational activities, community activities with reference to the organisation of post literacy programmes to the rural people.

Objectives of the Study

(i) To develop an instrument to measure the role performance of adult/continuing education workers.

(ii) To study the influence of sex, age, educational qualification and community background on the role-performance of adult/continuing education workers.

(iii) To study the influence of sex, age, educational qualification and community background of the Adult/continuing education workers on their attitude towards adult education.

(iv) To know the influence of adult/continuing education workers attitude towards adult education on their role performance.

(v) To examine how the personality characteristics are related to the role performance of adult/continuing education workers.

Hypotheses

In the light of the above objectives, the following hypotheses are framed the testing.

(i) There exists significant difference in the role performance of the adult/continuing education workers due to variation in their sex.

(ii) There exists significant difference in the role performance of the adult/continuing education workers due to variation in their age.

(iii) There exists significant difference in the role performance of adult/continuing education workers due to variation in their education qualification.

(iv) There exists significant difference in the role performance of adult/continuing education workers due to variation in their community.

(v) There is significant difference in the attitude of adult/continuing education workers towards adult education due to variation in their sex.

(vi) There is significant difference in the attitude of adult/continuing education workers towards adult education due to variations in their age, educational qualification and community background.

(vii) There is a significant difference among Adult/continuing education workers representing different levels of positive attitude and their role performance.

(viii) There is significant difference among the adult/continuing education workers representing different levels of scoring in each one of the 16 Personality Factors (as measured by Cattels 16 P.F.) and their role performance.

Need and Importance of the Study

Illiteracy is one of the major problems of a country. To boost literacy and post literacy programmes, the Government of India started National Literacy Mission on May, 1988. For promoting post literacy and continuing education for neo-literates and school dropouts, a good number of post literacy centres were started throughout the country as a part of National Literacy Mission. To carryout the post literacy and continuing educational activities, the post literacy workers have been appointed. The post literacy or continuing education worker is not limited to instruction but also expected to play a predominant role to activate the community to take up developmental tasks in that community. In other words, we may say, for proper functioning of the continuing education centres the instructor has to play three major roles i.e. teaching roles, organising roles and community roles. The efficiency or performance of the continuing education worker to a larger extent depends on how effectively he/she discharges the roles expected of him/her.

In the performance of the above stated roles, several factors may come into the way of continuing education worker such as age, sex, educational qualification and community.

The other factors such as the attitude of continuing education worker towards adult education will also influence his role performance. Apart from the above the continuing education workers performance may also be influenced by his personality. Personality is the variable that has the potential of influencing how a continuing education workers should go about in discharging different roles expected to him effectively. Several researches conducted in formal system of education have also indicated that the personality characteristics influence significantly the teaching effectiveness. Hence, one can safely come to the conclusion that the personality of an individual can play a dominant role in determining his/her role performance.

In the light of the above, variations in sex, age, educational qualification and community, attitude and type of personality characteristics possessed by the adult/continuing education workers may significantly influence their role performance as adult/continuing education workers. Researches focusing on the above aspects are of vital importance to understand the concept of role vital importance to understand the concept of role performance and the factor influencing the same. The present study is an attempt in this direction.

Limitations of the Study

The study is limited to the Adult/continuing education workers working in the post literacy projects in Tamil Nadu. The study is limited to identify the role performance of the Preraks under the three major roles namely—teaching role, organisational role and community role. A five point role performance scale is used to collect the responses from the subjects. Role performance has been assessed in this study through self-ratings, community ratings, neo-literate ratings and cumulative ratings. A five point attitude scale and cattle 16 P.F. Questionnaire are the only instruments used to study the attitude of continuing education workers towards adult education and personality of the continuing education workers, respectively.

The methodology used in the present study is explained in the succeeding chapter.

4
Methodology

Introduction

There are different methods to be followed at the various stages of any investigation. The details of such methods followed in this study are; construction of research tools, sample frame, collection of data, scoring of the instruments and various statistical methods employed in the analysis of data.

Construction of Tools

(i) Adult/Continuing Education Workers Role Performance Scale

For the purpose of the study, the adult/continuing education workers role performance scale is developed. This scale consists of three major roles namely—teaching roles, organisation roles and community roles. Under reach major role, several activities to be performed by the adult/continuing education workers are listed out in the form of statements. The statements are so framed and there are no ambiguity and repetitions. There are 17 statements consisting of teaching roles, 10 statements consisting of organising roles and 9 statements consisting of community roles, altogether 36 in number. Each statement can be rated on any of the five categories namely "very difficult to perform, difficult to perform, moderately performed, easily performed and very easy to perform" having the scores, 1, 2, 3, 4, 5 respectively. In view of this, the score of the adult/continuing education worker on the role performance ranges between 36 and 180 points. The role performance scores are derived for each adult continuing education worker through self ratings, community ratings, neo-literate ratings and cumulative ratings. To obtain neo-literate rating on adult/continuing education worker role performance, the mean of the ratings given by two chosen neo-literates on the role performance scale was calculated. Similarly, for each adult/continuing educating workers, one community leader rating score is taken. The mean performance score of the adult/continuing education workers is obtained through self-ratings. The ratings of the neo-literate, community and self-ratings are added to get the mean effectiveness score of the adult/continuing education workers. The reliability and validity of the scale is established by using the split half reliability. The obtained reliability of the tool is 72. With regard to validity—content validity, item validity and intrinsic validity are established.

(ii) Attitude Scale to Measure the Attitude of Adult/Continuing Education Workers

An attitude scale is developed by the investigator to measure the attitude of adult/continuing education workers towards the various aspects of adult education programme. The scale consists of 30 statement having both positive and negative indicators. Each statement can be rated on any of the 5 response categories i.e., "Strongly agree, Agree, undecided, Disagree and strongly disagree which carries numerical value 5, 4, 3, 2 and 1 respectively for positive statement, and numerical values 1, 2, 3, 4 and 5 respectively for negative statements. The score of the adult/continuing education worker will range between 30 and 150 points. The attitude scale is found to be highly reliable (0.69) and content validity, item validity and intrinsic validity are also established.

(iii) Personality Questionnaire

Cattle's 16 Personality Factor Form-E is adopted for use in the present study as it has number of advantages over other forms of personality test. There is increasing evidence accumulating from the studies using 16 P.F. to indicate that the total picture of personality using all the 16 P.F. is a better predictor than what may be obtained from the single scale lists. Moreover, 16 P.F are essentially independent factors and the correlation among them are usually negligible. The elementary vocabulary used in the test is easily understandable. Further, the test has an index to guard any motivational distortion that may be present. The test is translated into Tamil with the help of language and psychology experts. The reliability indices for both the versions of English and Tamil varied between 0.85 to 0.95. Further, the Tamil version thus obtained is also subjected to test, retest reliability by administering it to 30 adult/continuing education workers with an interval of 20 days. The reliability indices for this is ranged between 0.83 to 0.73. The procedure of administration and scoring of the 16 P. F Questionnaire Form E is the same as indicated in the manual.

Apart from the above three tests, the personal information related to the adult/continuing education worker such as—sex, age, educational qualifications and community background are collected.

Sample Frame

For the purpose of the study, the investigator requires three types of respondents namely—Adult/Continuing Education Workers, Community Leaders and Neo-literates. As a part of National Literacy Mission, total literacy and post literacy programmes are in operation in various districts of Tamil Nadu. In the first stage, the investigator selected 2 post literacy districts i.e. Madurai and Tanjore by using random sampling technique from among the various post literacy districts of Tamil Nadu. In both these districts, post literacy programmes are in operation at the time of conducting this investigation. At the second stage, the investigator selected 50 Adult/Continuing Education Workers from each post literacy district by using stratified random sampling technique considering their sex, age, educational status and community background as stratas. In the third stage, two neo-literates under each adult continuing education worker will be selected thus totalling 200 neo-literates of the study. Similarly, one community representative, representing the same will form the sample of the study. Thus the total sample consists of 100 adult/continuing education workers, 200 neo-literates and 100 community leaders.

Collection of Data

The required data is collected from the selected sample by administering the following tools to the following sample :

i) The role-performance scale is administered to the adult/continuing education workers to get self ratings.

ii) Community Representatives to get community rating.

iii) Neo-literates for neo-literate ratings.

iv) The ratings of above three groups form cumulative ratings.

v) A Five point attitude scale is administered on adult/continuing education workers to know their attitude towards various aspects of adult education programme.

vi) Cattle's 16 P.F Form-E is administered on adult/continuing education workers to get their score on 16 P.F.

Similarly, the personal information such as—sex, age, educational background and community of the adult/continuing education workers is collected from them. The data thus obtained is analysed by using mean, standard deviation, t-test and F-ratio.

5
Results and Discussion

Introduction

This chapter consists of two sections. Section-I deals with the analysis of influence of sex, age, educational background and community background on the role performance of the adult continuing education workers. Section-II deals with the impact of psychological factors on the role performance of adult continuing education workers.

Section I

In this section, the effect of certain variables of the adult continuing education workers on their role performance is studied. In order to study the influence of their variables, the adult continuing education workers are categorised into different groups and compared with respect to their obtained mean performance score based on different sources of rating, by using appropriate statistical technique like 't'-test.

Sex Vs. Adult/Continuing Education Workers Role Performance

In order to study the influence of sex on the role performance of adult continuing education worker, the sample are divided into men and women.

The 't'-test is employed to study the differences if any, between the mean role performance scores obtained by men and women instructors on various sources of ratings.

Table 5.1 shows the mean role performance scores, standard deviations and 't'-values obtained by men and women adult continuing education workers on all the four types of rating (self, community, neo-literates and cumulative).

The mean performance scores obtained through the self, community, neo-literate and cumulative ratings on adult continuing

Table 5.1 : Mean and SD of the Role-Performance Scores of Men and Women Adult/Continuing Education Workers on Different Sources of Ratings and the Calculated t-Values.

Source of Role Performance Scores	*Men (N=52)*		*Women (N=48)*		*Calculated t-value*
	Mean	*SD*	*Mean*	*SD*	
Self Ratings	124.85	16.94	125.52	19.90	0.178@
Community Ratings	111.80	13.71	117.35	13.67	2.020*
Neo-Literate Ratings	92.51	9.59	92.67	9.28	0.112@
Cumulative Ratings	105.92	18.75	107.05	20.06	0.840@

* Significant at 0.05 level
@ Not significant at 0.05 level

education worker, clearly shows that women are found to be more effective in performing their roles. The calculated 't'-value with respect to community ratings is significant at 0.05 level indicating the better performance of women. Hence, the formulated hypothesis "there exists significant difference in the adult continuing education workers in their sex" is accepted with respect to community ratings only.

Even though, the 't' value is not significant with respect of self, neo-literate and cumulative ratings, the obtained mean values clearly indicates the better performance of women workers than men.

Age Vs. Adult/Continuing Education Workers Role Performance

Based on Age, the adult continuing education workers are categorised into three groups (21–30, 31–40, 41–50 years) to study the influence of age on the role-performance of adult continuing education workers. The difference among the mean performance scores of different age groups of adult continuing education workers are studied by applying 'F'-test. The mean performance scores, standard deviation and F-values obtained by the different age group of workers on all types of ratings are shown in Table 5.2.

As obtained F-value with respect to self-rating is significant 0.05 level, indicating the influence of different age group on the role-performance of Adult/Continuing Education Workers. Hence, the formulated hypothesis "there exists significant difference in the role performance of adult continuing education workers due to variation in their age" is accepted with respect to self-ratings only. The mean

Table 5.2 : Mean and SD of the Role-Performance Scores of Different Age Group of Adult/Continuing Education Workers on Different Sources of Ratings and the Calculated F-Values.

Source of Role Performance Scores	*Age Groups*						*Calculated F-value*
	21 – 30 (N = 45)		*31 – 40 (N = 36)*		*41 – 50 (N = 19)*		
	Mean	*SD*	*Mean*	*SD*	*Mean*	*SD*	
Self Ratings	129.11	16.66	124.91	18.51	116.36	19.79	3.38*
Community Ratings	113.06	16.33	116.08	11.80	114.66	11.39	0.473@
Neo-Literate Ratings	94.17	10.71	90.91	8.16	91.94	7.75	2.53@
Cumulative Ratings	107.55	20.15	103.88	19.43	103.58	17.22	1.14@

* Significant at 0.05 level
@ Not significant at 0.05 level

values obtained by the different age group workers reveal that the younger workers (21–30) are better in their role performance than the workers with 31–40 age group and 41–50 age group.

On the other hand, the F-values obtained with respect to community, neo-literate and cumulative ratings are not significant at 0.05 level.

Educational Qualification vs. the Role Performance of Adult/ Continuing Education Workers

The sample adult continuing education workers are categorised into three group i.e., 10th std., Higher Secondary and Graduation. The three types of Adult/Continuing Education Workers representing different levels of education are compared in their role performance scores by using F-test.

The mean effectiveness scores, standard deviation and the F-values obtained by the adult continuing education workers representing different educational qualification in different ratings are presented in Table 5.3.

The mean performance scores obtained by different education groups on different sources of rating and the obtained F-values are

Table 5.3 : Mean and SD of the Role-Performance Scores of Adult/Continuing Education Workers with Different Sources of Ratings and the Calculated F-Values

Source of Role Performance Scores	*Educational Qualification*						*Calculated F-value*
	10th Std. (N = 31)		*Hr. Sec. (N = 45)*		*Graduation (N = 24)*		
	Mean	*SD*	*Mean*	*SD*	*Mean*	*SD*	
Self Ratings	113.54	19.10	122.66	11.61	144.91	10.55	34.47**
Community Ratings	110.06	9.73	113.04	15.47	122.44	12.47	6.55**
Neo-Literate Ratings	88.96	5.26	91.63	8.24	99.08	12.21	19.48**
Cumulative Ratings	100.38	16.09	104.69	17.61	116.44	22.39	21.68**

Note : * Significant at 0.05 level

significant at 0.01 level. Hence, the formulated hypothesis "there is significant difference in the role performance of adult continuing education workers due to variations in their educational qualification" is accepted with respect to all types of ratings. Further, the trend of the mean performance scores reveal that the adult continuing education workers with graduate qualification are performing their role more effectively.

Community Vs. Role Performance of Adult/Continuing Education Workers

In order to study the impact of the community background of the adult continuing education workers on their role performance, the sample are divided into three groups namely-adult continuing education workers belonging to B.C, MBC and SC communities. F-test is applied to findout the difference if any, among different community groups in their mean performance scores.

Table 5.4 indicates the mean performance scores, Standard Deviations and F-values obtained by the Adult Continuing Education Workers representing different community groups.

The trend of the mean performance scores demonstrate that the Adult Continuing Education Workers belonging to Backward Community are rated as more effective workers by all the raters. However,

Table 5.4 : Mean and SD of the Role Performance Adult/ Continuing Education Workers with Different Community Background Based on Difference Sources of Ratings and the Calculated F-value

Source of Role Performance Scores	*Community*						*Calculated F-value*
	B.C. (N = 38)		*M.B.C. (N = 29)*		*S.C. (N = 33)*		
	Mean	*SD*	*Mean*	*SD*	*Mean*	*SD*	
Self Ratings	130.63	17.49	127.00	17.89	117.30	17.41	5.29*
Community Ratings	114.78	15.19	111.62	14.11	116.60	12.03	1.00@
Neo-Literate Ratings	95.78	9.78	92.42	9.73	88.12	6.73	13.65*
Cumulative Ratings	109.07	19.79	106.59	19.34	102.53	18.47	4.13

* Significant at 0.05 level
@ Not significant

only the community ratings show that there is no significant difference between the instructors representing different community groups in their role performance scores. But the other raters show that there is significant difference between the adult continuing education workers representing different communal groups in their role performance scores. Hence, the stated hypothesis "there exists significant difference in the role performance of adult continuing education workers due to variations in their community" is accepted with respect to self, neo-literate and cumulative ratings.

Section II
Impact of Psychological Factors on the Role Performance of Adult/Continuing Education Workers

Influence of Sex, Age, Educational Qualification and Community on the Attitude of Adult/Continuing Education Workers

In this part, the effect of variables sex, age, educational qualification and community of the adult continuing education workers on their attitude towards adult education are studied. In order to study the influence of these variables on the attitude of adult continuing education workers, they are divided into different groups and are compared with respect of their obtained mean attitude scores. T-test and F-test are applied to know the significant difference between the groups and among the groups respectively.

Sex Vs. the Attitude of Adult/Continuing Education Workers

Table 5.5 shows the mean attitude scores, standard deviations and F-values obtained by mean and women adult continuing education workers.

Table 5.5 : Mean and SD of Attitude Scores by Mean and Women Adult/Continuing Education Workers towards Literacy Programmes and the Calculated 't' Values

Variable	*Mean*	*SD*	*Calculated t-value*
Men (N = 52)	86.57	4.30	.55@
Women (N = 48)	86.06	4.96	

@ : Not significant at 0.05 level

In Table 5.5, the obtained 't' value is not significant indicating the non-influence of sex on the attitude of adult continuing education workers towards adult education. Hence, the formulated hypothesis "there is significant difference in the attitude of adult and continuing education workers towards adult education programme due to variations in their sex" is rejected.

Age, Educational Qualification and Community Vs. the Attitude of Adult/Continuing Education Workers

Table 5.6 shows the mean attitude scores, standard deviations and the calculated 'F'-values obtained by the different age group, educational qualification and community groups of adult continuing education workers.

The obtained F-value with respect to the age group (1.26), education qualification (1.69) and Community groups (1.10) are not significant at 0.05 level indicating the non-influence of these variables on the attitude of adult continuing education workers towards adult education Programme. Hence, the formulated hypothesis "there is significant difference in the attitude of adult continuing education workers towards adult education due to the variations in their age, education qualification and community background" is rejected.

Table 5.5 : Mean and SD of Attitude Scores by Mean and Women Adult/Continuing Education Workers towards Literacy Programmes and the Calculated 't' Values

Variable	*Mean Attitude Score*	*SD*	*Calculated F-value*
Age Group			
21–30 (N=45)	86.02	5.15	
31–40 (N=37)	85.94	4.21	1.26@
41–50 (N=18)	87.88	3.81	
Educational Qualification			
10th Std. (N=31)	87.58	3.49	
Hr. Sec. (N=45)	85.80	4.77	1.69@
Graduation (N=24)	85.70	5.40	
Community			
BC (N=38)	86.23	4.46	
MBC (N=29)	87.31	3.73	1.10@
SC (N=33)	85.57	5.40	

@ : Not significant at 0.05 level

Adult/Continuing Education Workers Attitude Towards Adult Education Vs. Role Performance

In order to study the impact of Adult Continuing Education workers attitude towards adult education on their role performance, the sample of adult continuing education workers are categorised into three groups i.e. adult continuing education workers possessing low, medium and high positive attitude based on the criteria near ±1/2 SD. The three groups of adult continuing education workers are compared in terms of their obtained mean performance score to find out the significant difference between these groups.

The mean performance scores, SDs obtained by the adult continuing education workers, low, medium and high positive attitude groups based on the four types of ratings and the respective F-values are presented in Table 5.7.

From the Table 5.7, it is evident that the Adult/Continuing Education Workers possessing low, medium and high positive attitude towards adult education differ significantly in their mean performance scores as per neo-literate ratings. However, as per the other source

Table 5.7 : Mean and SD of the Role Performance Scores obtained by the Adult/Continuing Education Workers with Low, Medium and High Positive Attitude Towards Literacy Programme and the Calculated F-value

Source of Role Performance Scores	*Level of Attitude*						*Calculated F-value*
	Low (N = 30)		*Medium (N = 31)*		*High (N = 39)*		
	Mean	*SD*	*Mean*	*SD*	*Mean*	*SD*	
Self Ratings	124.76	16.59	122.16	18.42	128.83	20.28	1.02@
Community Ratings	114.60	15.32	114.51	13.21	114.33	13.66	.003@
Neo-Literate Ratings	91.13	8.36	90.27	6.09	96.13	12.26	6.82*
Cumulative Ratings	108.92	20.55	104.30	18.70	105.63	18.88	1.85@

* Significant at 0.01 level
@ Not significant at 0.05 level

ratings, i.e., self, community and cumulative ratings the difference between these groups are not statistically significant. Hence, the hypothesis "there is significant difference between adult continuing education workers representing the different levels of positive attitude possessed in their role performance" is rejected in case of self, community and cumulative ratings. Further, it is noted that the adult continuing education workers with high level of attitude performed their roles more effectively than the adult education workers with low, medium positive attitudes. The trend of the mean performance scores shows that higher the positive attitude, higher will be the role performance of the adult continuing education workers. But, it is reverse in case of cumulative ratings.

Personality Vs. Role Performance of Adult/Continuing Education Workers

In order to study the influence of personality on the role performance of adult continuing education workers, the Cattle's-16 Personality Factor Questionnaire is adopted to suit the needs of the study. The adult continuing education workers are classified into three groups based on the scores obtained by each one of the personality factor by using the criteria mean ±1/2 SD. Based on this criteria, the sample of adult/continuing education workers are classified as low, medium and top scores on each one of the personality factors and the corresponding mean performance scores of these three groups. These three groups are compared by using ANOVA test to bring out the influence of personality factors on adult continuing education workers role-performance based on the four sources of ratings. The obtained results are interpreted to bring the relationship between various personality factors and role-performance of the adult continuing education workers.

Factor-A

The person who scores low on Factor A tends to be stiff, cool, aloof, working alone and avoidance of clash of view points. He likes things rather than people. He is likely to be precise and rigid in his way of doing things. A person who scores high on this factors tends to be good natured, easy going, ready to cooperate, attentive to people, soft hearted, mindful, trustful and adoptable.

The mean performance scores, standard deviations and F-value of the continuing education workers of low, medium and top scoring groups on Factor-A on all four sources of rating are shown in Table 5.8.

Table 5.8 : Mean and SD of the Role Performance Scores obtained by the Adult/Continuing Education Workers with Low, Medium and High Positive Attitude Towards Literacy Programme and the Calculated F-value

Source of Role Performance Scores	*Low (N = 27)*		*Medium (N = 32)*		*High (N = 41)*		*Calculated F-value*
	MRPS	*SD*	*MRPS*	*SD*	*MRPS*	*SD*	
Self Ratings	120.00	17.68	126.63	18.75	127.60	18.18	1.52@
Community Ratings	112.92	12.42	113.06	14.34	116.58	14.52	.80@
Neo-Literate Ratings	91.37	7.95	95.04	12.29	91.48	7.81	3.25*
Cumulative Ratings	103.91	17.41	107.39	19.68	106.79	20.35	1.07@

* Significant at 0.05 level
@ Not significant

From Table 5.8 it is observed that the calculated F-values are less than table value with respect to self, community and cumulative ratings. On the other hand, the F-value is significant with respect to neo-literate ratings indicating the significant difference between the mean performance scores of adult continuing education workers representing low, medium and top scores. Hence the formulated hypothesis is accepted with respect to neo-literates ratings only.

Factor-B

The person scoring low on Factor-B tends to be slow to learn and grasp, dull and sluggish. He tends to have low task or capacity for the higher forms of knowledge and to be somewhat borrish. On the other hand, the top scorers on Factor-B tends to be quick to grasp ideas, a fast learner and intelligent. He is usually rather cultured.

The mean performance scores, standard deviations and F-values obtained by the adult continuing education workers representing low, medium and top scoring groups on Factor-B on all sources of ratings are shown in Table 5.9.

Table 5.9 : Mean and SD of the Role Performance Scores obtained by Low, Medium and Top Scores on Factor-B and their Respectively 'F' values

FACTOR-B

Source of Role Performance Scores	*Low (N = 31)*		*Medium (N = 43)*		*Top (N = 26)*		*Calculated F-value*
	MRPS	*SD*	*MRPS*	*SD*	*MRPS*	*SD*	
Self Ratings	124.45	14.60	125.53	20.67	125.46	19.93	0.34@
Community Ratings	114.00	11.90	111.62	15.30	119.73	12.55	2.88@
Neo-Literate Ratings	90.30	8.58	94.74	11.47	91.76	4.92	4.40*
Cumulative Ratings	104.76	18.65	106.66	19.72	107.18	19.76	.520@

* Significant at 0.05 level
@ Not significant

From Table 5.9, it is evident that the obtained F-value with respect to neo-literate ratings is significant at 0.05 level, indicating the significant difference in the performance of adult continuing education workers representing low, medium and top scorers on Factor-B. On the other hand, the F-values are not significant with respect to self, community and cumulative ratings which indicates the non-influence of Factor-B on adult continuing education workers role performance. Further, the trend of the mean performance scores obtained by the three groups of adult continuing education workers indicating that the top scores are rated as more effective workers. The low scorers are rated as low performers as per the self-ratings, community ratings and cumulative ratings. Neo-literates rating shows that the medium scores on Factor-B were the better role performers than the top and low scorers.

Factor-C

The person who scores low on Factor-C tends to be emotionally immature, lack in frustration, tolerance, changeable, evasive, neurotically fatigue and easily annoyed. The high scorers on this factor tends to be emotionally matured, stable, calm, mature, possessive ego strength and possessing high group morale.

The mean performance scores, standard deviations, and obtained F-value of the adult continuing education workers representing low, medium and top scores on Factor-C on all four sources of ratings are shown in Table 5.10.

Table 5.10 : Mean and SD of the Role Performance Scores obtained by Low, Medium and Top Scores on Factor-C and their Respectively 'F' values

FACTOR-C

Source of Role Performance Scores	*Low (N = 31)*		*Medium (N = 43)*		*Top (N = 26)*		*Calculated F-value*
	MRPS	*SD*	*MRPS*	*SD*	*MRPS*	*SD*	
Self Ratings	126.03	14.93	123.43	19.36	124.18	19.87	0.79@
Community Ratings	116.34	11.09	112.85	16.75	115.00	12.03	.532@
Neo-Literate Ratings	93.28	8.62	91.97	9.20	92.81	10.34	.333@
Cumulative Ratings	107.24	18.14	105.56	20.21	106.18	19.39	.237@

* Significant at 0.05 level
@ Not significant

The obtained F-value in Table 5.10 were less than the table value with respect to all four types of ratings. It means that the adult continuing education workers representing low, medium and top scorers on Factor-C do not differ significantly in their mean performance scores. Hence the formulated hypothesis is rejected.

Factor-E

The person who scores low on Factor-E tends to be dependent, a follower and to action which goes along with the group. He tends to lean on others in making decisions and is often soft-hearted, expressive and easily upset. Whereas the individual scoring high on Factor-E tends to be ascendant, self-assumed, perspective, independent minded and hold in his approach to the situations. He may at times be hard, stern, hostile, soleman, tuff minded and authoritarian.

Table 5.11 shows the mean performance scores, standard deviation and F-values obtained by adult/continuing education workers, representing low, medium and top scorers on Factor-E on all four sources of ratings.

Table 5.11 : Mean and SD of the Role Performance Scores obtained by Low, Medium and Top Scores on Factor-E and their Respectively 'F' values

FACTOR-E

Source of Role Performance Scores	*Low (N = 31)*		*Medium (N = 42)*		*Top (N = 27)*		*Calculated F-value*
	MRPS	*SD*	*MRPS*	*SD*	*MRPS*	*SD*	
Self Ratings	128.32	17.80	124.19	18.82	123.11	18.38	.684@
Community Ratings	114.19	13.38	115.97	14.87	114.74	13.07	.662@
Neo-Literate Ratings	94.51	14.53	92.01	5.87	91.14	5.13	2.05@
Cumulative Ratings	107.38	20.62	106.09	19.07	105.03	18.48	.427@

@ Not significant at 0.05 level

It is evident from Table 5.11 that the calculated F-values are less than the table value in case of all types of ratings indicating that the adult continuing education workers representing low, medium and top scorers on Factor-E is not significantly differ in their mean performance scorers. Even though significant difference are not found, the trend of the mean performance scores obtained by adult continuing education workers representing low, medium and top scorers shows that the self-ratings, neo-literate and cumulative ratings are rated the low scoring adult continuing education workers on Factor-E as more effective role performers. As per community ratings, the medium scorers were found to be better performers in their roles.

Factor - F

The person who scores low on Factor-F tends to be taciturn, reticent, introspective. He is sometimes incommunicative, melancholic, anxious, depressed, smug, languid and slow whereas, a person who scores high on this factor tends to be cheerful, frank, expressive, quick, alert and unperturbed. He is frequently chosen as elected leader.

The mean performance scores, standard deviations and F-values obtained by the adult continuing education workers representing low, medium and top score groups on Factor-F from all the four types of ratings are presented in Table 5.12.

Table 5.12 : Mean and SD of the Role Performance Scores obtained by Low, Medium and Top Scorers on Factor-G and their Respectively 'F' values

FACTOR-F

Source of Role Performance Scores	*Low (N = 46)*		*Medium (N = 25)*		*Top (N = 29)*		*Calculated F-value*
	MRPS	*SD*	*MRPS*	*SD*	*MRPS*	*SD*	
Self Ratings	126.93	13.81	129.48	18.12	119.00	23.70	2.58@
Community Ratings	114.54	12.58	114.12	15.68	114.65	14.77	.010@
Neo-Literate Ratings	92.13	7.70	93.82	11.05	92.27	10.41	.563
Cumulative Ratings	106.36	18.30	107.81	20.67	104.55	19.95	.771@

@ Not significant at 0.05 level

Table 5.12 indicates that the calculated F-values are less than the table value. In other words, the difference between the mean performance scores of the three groups of adult continuing education workers based on different sources of ratings are not significant. However, the trend of the mean performance scores shows that the medium scorers on this factor are found to be better role performance as per the self, neo-literate and cumulative ratings. In contrast to the above, top scorers by the community ratings are better role performers.

Factor-G

A person who scores low on Factor-G tends to be Fickle minded, not dependable, irresolute, unsteady, quitting, sometimes he is demanding impatient, indolent, obstructive, lacking in internal standards. On the contrary, a person who scores high on this factor tends to be strong in character, preserving, responsible, determined, consistent, planful, energetic, cautious and well organised. He is usually conscientious, with regard for moral standards and prefers efficient people to other companions.

The mean performance scores, standard deviations and obtained F-values by the adult continuing education workers representing low, medium and top scorers on Factor-G from all sources of ratings are shown in Table 5.13.

Table 5.13 : Mean and SD of the Role Performance Scores obtained by Low, Medium and Top Scorers on Factor-G and their Respectively 'F' values

FACTOR-G

Source of Role Performance Scores	*Low*		*Medium*		*Top*		*Calculated F-value*
	MRPS	*SD*	*MRPS*	*SD*	*MRPS*	*SD*	
Self Ratings	124.12	18.92	122.88	19.81	128.48	16.27	.790@
Community Ratings	116.19	13.37	107.11	16.24	118.46	9.90	5.96**
Neo-Literate Ratings	93.39	7.60	93.12	12.81	92.40	8.23	.117@
Cumulative Ratings	106.27	19.03	104.06	19.82	107.93	19.44	1.17@

** Significant at 0.01 level
@ Not significant at 0.05 level

The results of Anova in Table 5.13, clearly indicate that there is significant difference between the mean performance scores obtained by the adult continuing education workers representing low, medium and top scorers on Factor-G, as per community ratings. However, there are no significant difference among the mean performance scores of three group of adult continuing education workers from other sources of ratings, i.e., self, neo-literate and cumulative ratings. The trend of the mean effectiveness scores obtained by the three groups on Factor-G do not indicate any clear trend, The low scorers are rated as better role performers by the neo-literates. The top scorers are found to be better role performers as per self-ratings, community and cumulative ratings.

Factor-H

The person who scores low on Factor-H tends to be shy, withdrawing, cautious, and cool. He usually has inferiority feelings. He tends to be slow and impeded in speech and unexpressing himself, dislike occupation with personal contacts, prefers one or two close friends in large group and is not able to keep in contact with all that is going on around him. On the other hand, a person who scores high on this Factor, tends to be sociable, participating, spontaneous, abundant in emotional response and ready to try new things. He is able to face wear and fear in dealing with people and grueling emotional situations without fatigue.

Table 5.14 represents the mean performance scores, standard deviations and F-values obtained by adult/continuing education workers representing low, medium and top scores on Factor-H, based on all sources of ratings.

Table 5.14 : Mean and SD of the Role Performance Scores obtained by Low, Medium and Top Scorers on Factor-H and their respective 'F' values

FACTOR-H

Source of Role Performance Scores	*Low (N = 44)*		*Medium (N = 25)*		*Top (N = 33)*		*Calculated F-value*
	MRPS	*SD*	*MRPS*	*SD*	*MRPS*	*SD*	
Self Ratings	126.93	17.31	123.30	19.90	120.15	18.88	.368@
Community Ratings	117.13	11.75	110.78	15.48	113.48	15.07	1.77@
Neo-Literate Ratings	93.05	9.52	93.53	10.64	91.34	8.34	.893@
Cumulative Ratings	107.54	19.38	105.27	19.22	105.08	19.53	.747@

@ Not significant at 0.05 level

In Table 5.14 it is seen that the difference between the mean performance scores of adult continuing education workers representing low, medium and top scoring groups on Factor-H are not statistically significant from all sources of ratings. In other words, the influence of personality Factor-H on the role performance of adult continuing education workers is minimum. However, the mean performance scores from all sources of ratings indicate that the low scorers on this factor are better role-performers as per self, community and cumulative ratings. On the other hand, the neo-literate rating indicates that medium scorers are performing their role effectively than the top and low scorers.

Factor–I

The person who scores low on Factor-I tends to be practical, realistic, masculine, independent, responsible, but uncultured. He is sometimes phlegmatic, hard, cynical, smug. He tends to keep a group operating on a practical and realistic 'no nonsense basis'. On the other hand, a person who scores high on this factor tends to be tender minded, imaginative, introspective, artistic, fastidious, excitable. He is sometimes demanding, impatient, impractical. He dislikes crude people and rough occupations. He tends to slowup group performance and to upset group moral by negative remarks.

In Table 5.15, the mean performance scores, standard deviations and the respective F-value obtained by the adult continuing education workers representing low, medium and top scorers on Factor-I based on all sources of rating were presented.

Table 5.15 : Mean and SD of the Role Performance Scores obtained by Low, Medium and Top Scorers on Factor-I and their respective 'F' values

FACTOR-I

Source of Role Performance Scores	*Low (N = 29)*		*Medium (N = 47)*		*Top (N = 24)*		*Calculated F-value*
	MRPS	*SD*	*MRPS*	*SD*	*MRPS*	*SD*	
Self Ratings	125.65	14.55	124.59	21.25	125.95	16.83	.044@
Community Ratings	115.55	13.45	114.21	14.23	113.66	14.31	.133@
Neo-Literate Ratings	91.53	6.56	94.89	10.82	90.93	9.12	2.23@
Cumulative Ratings	106.06	18.52	106.75	19.84	105.32	19.67	.175@

@ Not significant at 0.05 level

The obtained result in Table 5.15, clearly shows that the difference between the mean performance scores obtained by the adult continuing education workers belonging to low, medium and top scoring group from all sources of rating are not significant either at 0.05 level or 0.01 level. The trend of the mean performance scores indicate that the adult continuing education workers representing top scoring group had obtained more mean performance scores as per the self ratings. On the other hand, medium scoring group adult continuing education workers are found to be better in performing their roles as per neo-literate and cumulative ratings. The community ratings reveal that the low scorers on this factor are performing their role effectively.

Factor-L

The person who score low on Factor-L tends to be free of jealous tendencies, adaptable, cheerful, composed, concerned about other people and also a good team worker. Whereas a person who scores high on this factor tends to be mistrusting and doubtful. He is often involve in his own ego, self-opinionated, and interested internal mental life. He is usually deliberate in his actions, unconcerned about other people and a poor team member.

In Table 5.16 the mean performance scores, standard deviations and the respective F-values obtained by the adult continuing education workers representing low, medium and top scorers on Factor-L based on all sources of ratings are presented.

Table 5.16 : Mean and SD of the Role Performance Scores obtained by Low, Medium and Top Scorers on Factor-L and their respective 'F' values

FACTOR-L

Source of Role Performance Scores	*Low (N = 37)*		*Medium (N = 32)*		*Top (N = 31)*		Calculated F-value
	MRPS	*SD*	*MRPS*	*SD*	*MRPS*	*SD*	
Self Ratings	129.21	17.29	127.09	19.77	118.38	18.58	3.35*
Community Ratings	115.70	13.44	115.50	14.78	111.93	13.63	.743@
Neo-Literate Ratings	93.62	11.04	94.39	9.97	89.30	4.97	5.93**
Cumulative Ratings	108.04	20.25	107.94	19.86	102.23	17.27	3.83**

** Significant at 0.01 level * Significant at 0.05 level

@ Not significant at 0.05 level

The results of F-test shows that the difference between the mean performance scores of adult continuing education workers representing low, medium and top scoring groups are not statistically significant as per community ratings. It indicates that the influence of Factor-L on the role performance of adult continuing education workers is not significant as per community ratings. On the other hand, the F-values are significant with reference to self, neo-literate and cumulative ratings. Further, the trend of the mean performance scores reveal that the mean performance scores of adult continuing education workers who scored low on Factor-L are high as per self, community and cumulative ratings. But, it is not true in case of neo-literate ratings. The medium scoring adult continuing education workers on Factor-L are performed their roles better as per the ratings of neo-literates.

Factor-M

The person who scores low on Factor-M tends to be anxious to do the right thing, practical and conformist. He is easily concerned but able to keep his head in emergency. He is often rather narrowly correct and unimaginative. Contrast to this a person who scores high on this factor tends to be unconventional, unconcerned, ego centric, sensitive and imaginative. He sometimes makes emotional senses, is somewhat irresponsible, impractical, undependable. He is often rejected in group situations.

The mean performance scores, standard deviations and the respective F-values by the adult continuing education workers on Factor-m based on all sources of ratings are shown in Table 5.17.

Table 5.17 : Mean and SD of the Role Performance Scores obtained by Low, Medium and Top Scorers on Factor-M and their respective 'F' values

FACTOR-M

Source of Role Performance Scores	*Low (N = 35)*		*Medium (N = 33)*		*Top (N = 34)*		*Calculated F-value*
	MRPS	*SD*	*MRPS*	*SD*	*MRPS*	*SD*	
Self Ratings	127.03	13.85	120.45	21.68	127.97	16.54	1.68@
Community Ratings	116.87	11.99	113.36	14.93	113.20	14.68	.735@
Neo-Literate Ratings	92.40	6.60	71.62	8.36	93.72	12.30	.840@
Cumulative Ratings	107.18	18.73	104.26	19.27	107.15	20.11	.991@

@ Not significant at 0.05 level

Results shows that the difference in the mean performance scores of the adult continuing workers represent low, medium and top scoring groups are not statistically significant at 0.05 level. It indicates that influence of Factor-M on adult continuing education works are not significant. Further, the trend of the mean performance scores indicates slight mean differences among the three groups and are not showing and definite direction.

Factor-N

The person who scores low on Factor-N tends to be unsophisticated, sentimental and simple. He is easily pleased and sometimes crude and awkward. Contrast to this a person who scores high on this factor tends to be polished, experienced, worldly, shrewd. He tends to be analytical. He has an intellectual unsentimental approach to situations.

Table 5.18 indicates the mean performance scores, standard deviations and respective F-values obtained by the adult continuing education workers representing low, medium and top scoring groups on Factor-N scores on all sources of ratings.

Table 5.18 : Mean and SD of the Role Performance Scores obtained by Low, Medium and Top Scorers on Factor-N and their respective 'F' values

FACTOR-N

Source of Role Performance Scores	*Low (N = 43)*		*Medium (N = 21)*		*Top (N = 36)*		*Calculated F-value*
	MRPS	*SD*	*MRPS*	*SD*	*MRPS*	*SD*	
Self Ratings	129.44	14.34	130.66	19.54	116.88	19.35	6.141**
Community Ratings	114.76	11.49	115.00	17.73	113.80	14.42	.064@
Neo-Literate Ratings	94.18	11.78	93.19	6.86	90.34	6.87	3.43*
Cumulative Ratings	108.14	19.36	108.01	19.08	102.84	18.01	3.42*

** Significant at 0.01 level * Significant at 0.05 level

@ Not significant at 0.05 level

The obtained F-values indicate that significant differences are found in the mean performance scores among the adult continuing education workers representing low, medium and top scoring groups on Factor-N, as per self, neo-literate and cumulative ratings. On the other hand, the mean performance scores of the three groups are not statistically significant as per community ratings. Further, the trend of the mean performance scores obtained by the three groups of adult continuing education workers on different sources of ratings also confirm that the low scoring groups have obtained better mean performance score as per neo-literate and cumulative ratings. On the other hand, the medium scoring group obtained more mean performance score as per self and community ratings.

Factor-O

The person who scores low on Factor-O tends to be palacial, calm with unshakeable nerve. He has a mature unanxious, confident, resilient and secure. On the other hand, the person who scores high tends to be depressed, moody, a women suspicious, brooding, child like anxious and does not feel accepted in groups or free to participate.

The mean performance scores, standard deviations, and respective F-values obtained by adult continuing education works representing low, medium and top scoring groups on Factor-O based all sources of ratings are shown in Table 5.19.

Table 5.19 : Mean and SD of the Role Performance Scores obtained by Low, Medium and Top Scorers on Factor-O and their respective 'F' values

FACTOR-O

Source of Role Performance Scores	*Low (N = 43)*		*Medium (N = 23)*		*Top (N = 39)*		*Calculated F-value*
	MRPS	*SD*	*MRPS*	*SD*	*MRPS*	*SD*	
Self Ratings	122.51	20.21	125.21	18.84	128.52	15.18	1.023@
Community Ratings	112.76	13.55	115.13	15.22	116.17	13.59	.599@
Neo-Literate Ratings	92.18	8.57	91.36	9.85	93.94	10.10	1.16@
Cumulative Ratings	104.91	18.89	105.77	20.31	108.14	19.35	1.08@

@ Not significant at 0.05 level

It can be seen from Table 5.19, that the difference between mean performance scores of low, medium and top scoring groups are not significant as the calculated F-values are less than the table value. It clearly indicates that the influence of Factor-O on adult continuing education workers role performance is not statistically significant.

Factor-Q_1

The person who scores low on Factor-Q_1 tends to be over cautious and moderate. He is opposed to any change, inclined to go along with tradition, and tends not be interested in analytical, intellectual thought. On the other hand, a person who scores high on this factor tends to be interested in intellectual matters and fundamental issues. He frequently takes an issue with ideas. He tends to be more well informed, less inclined to moralise and more inclined to experiment in life, generally more tolerant of inconvenience.

The Table 5.20 shows the mean effectiveness scores, standard deviations and respective F-values obtained by adult continuing education workers representing low, medium and top scoring groups as Factor-Q, based on different sources of ratings.

Table 5.20 : Mean and SD of the Role Performance Scores obtained by Low, Medium and Top Scorers on Factor-Q_1 and their respective 'F' values

FACTOR-Q_1

Source of Role Performance Scores	*Low (N = 40)*		*Medium (N = 30)*		*Top (N = 30)*		*Calculated F-value*
	MRPS	*SD*	*MRPS*	*SD*	*MRPS*	*SD*	
Self Ratings	126.07	21.53	124.96	18.96	124.20	13.86	.090@
Community Ratings	115.00	16.73	115.73	11.81	112.50	11.75	.448@
Neo-Literate Ratings	93.75	9.85	91.80	8.28	91.85	9.89	1.001@
Cumulative Ratings	107.14	20.60	106.07	19.16	105.10	17.98	.383@

@ Not significant at 0.05 level

The results of the F-test in Table 5.20 reveals that the difference in the performance scores of low, medium and top scoring groups on Factor-Q, are not statistically significant and the obtained F-values are less than the table value. It clearly demonstrate the non-influence of Factor-Q_1 on adult continuing education workers role performance.

However, the trend of the mean performance scores obtained by the three groups of adult continuing education workers based on different sources of rating shows that worker representing low scoring group are rated as better role performers by the self, neo-literate and cumulative ratings. On the other hand, community ratings shows that the medium scoring adult continuing education workers are performing their role effectively.

Factor-Q_2

The person who scores low on Factor-Q_2 prefers to work and make decisions with other people, depends on social approval and admiration. He too go along with the group and may be lacking in resolutions. Contrary to above, a person who score's high on this factor tends to be an independent, resolute, accustomed to going his own ways in making decisions and taking action on his own. He is not necessarily dominant, however, in his relations with others.

The mean effectiveness scores, SDs and the respective F-value obtained by instructors representing low, medium and top scoring groups on Factor-Q_2 based on all sources of rating are shown in Table 5.21.

Table 5.21 : Mean and SD of the Role Performance Scores obtained by Low, Medium and Top Scorers on Factor-Q_2 and their respective 'F' values

FACTOR-Q_2

Source of Role Performance Scores	*Low (N = 30)*		*Medium (N = 52)*		*Top (N = 8)*		*Calculated F-value*
	MRPS	*SD*	*MRPS*	*SD*	*MRPS*	*SD*	
Self Ratings	123.16	11.73	124.65	19.26	130.05	14.55	.836@
Community Ratings	116.93	14.01	112.07	14.73	117.27	10.10	1.627@
Neo-Literate Ratings	92.16	6.87	93.11	9.73	91.10	12.01	.343@
Cumulative Ratings	106.10	18.91	105.74	19.29	107.73	20.60	.285@

@ Not significant at 0.05 level

The obtained F-value in Table 5.21 are less than the Table value indicating that the mean difference among low, medium and top scorers on Factor-Q_2 are not statistically significant. It is a clear indication education workers role performance does not related with each other significantly. However, the trend of the mean performance scores show that the top scorers are rated as more effective by self, community and cumulative ratings. Whereas, neo-literate ratings shows that the medium scores on Factor-Q_2 are more effective than the other groups.

Factor - Q_3

The person who scores low on Factor-Q_3 tends to lack will, control and character stability. He is not too considerate, careful or conscientious. On the other hand, a person who scores high on this Factor tends to have strong control of his emotions and general behaviour is inclined to be considerate, careful and evidence what is commonly termed "self-respect". He sometime tends however to be obstinate.

The Table 5.22 indicates the mean performance scores, SDs and the respective F-value obtained by adult continuing education workers representing low, medium and top scoring groups on the distribution of Factor-Q_3 scores from all sources of ratings.

Table 5.22 : Mean and SD of the Role Performance Scores obtained by Low, Medium and Top Scorers on Factor-Q_3 and their respective 'F' values

FACTOR-Q_3

Source of Role Performance Scores	*Low (N = 33)*		*Medium (N = 49)*		*Top (N = 18)*		*Calculated F-value*
	MRPS	*SD*	*MRPS*	*SD*	*MRPS*	*SD*	
Self Ratings	128.42	19.10	122.34	17.16	126.94	19.80	.189@
Community Ratings	116.12	12.04	113.00	14.31	115.44	16.19	.545@
Neo-Literate Ratings	96.19	12.59	89.50	6.02	94.41	7.42	11.96**
Cumulative Ratings	109.23	19.84	103.58	16.74	107.80	19.55	3.67*

** Significant at 0.01 level * Significant at 0.05 level
@ Not significant at 0.05 level

In Table 5.22, the mean difference between the low, medium and top scoring groups are statistically significant with respect to neo-literate ratings and cumulative ratings. The results of the F-test also reveal that the obtained F-values are greater than the table value. Contrary to this, the obtained F-value with respect to self, community and cumulative ratings are not significant. However, the trend of the mean performance scores indicate that the top scoring group on Factor-Q_3 are performing their roles more effectively as per the self ratings. Whereas, the low scores are rated as better role performance by the community, neo-literate and cumulative ratings.

Factor-Q_4

The person who scores low on Factor-Q_4 tends to be calm, relaxed, composed and satisfied. Whereas a person who scores high on this factor tends to be tense, excitable, restless, tactful and impatient. He is often over fatigued, but unable to remain inactive. He takes a poor view of group unity, orderlines, leadership.

The mean performance scores, SDs and respective 'F' values obtained by adult continuing education workers representing low, medium and top scoring groups of the distribution of Factor-Q_4 scores from all sources of ratings are shown in Table 5.23.

Table 5.23 : Mean and SD of the Role Performance Scores obtained by Low, Medium and Top Scorers on Factor-Q_4 and their respective 'F' values

FACTOR-Q_4

Source of Role Performance Scores	*Low (N = 35)*		*Medium (N = 35)*		*Top (N = 30)*		*Calculated F-value*
	MRPS	*SD*	*MRPS*	*SD*	*MRPS*	*SD*	
Self Ratings	116.20	19.09	130.25	18.74	129.73	12.57	7.28**
Community Ratings	110.00	15.71	117.37	13.57	116.30	10.90	2.93@
Neo-Literate Ratings	91.40	9.69	95.42	10.66	90.68	6.45	5.16**
Cumulative Ratings	102.25	17.87	109.62	20.27	106.85	19.35	5.26**

** Significant at 0.01 level * Significant at 0.05 level
@ Not significant at 0.05 level

It is seen from Table 5.23 that the calculated F-values are more than the table value between the low, medium and top scoring groups on Factor-Q_4 in the case of self neo-literate and cumulative ratings.

Contradictory to the above, in case of community ratings, the mean difference is statistically not significant. The trend of the mean effectiveness scores clearly demonstrate that the medium scorers are obtained better mean performance scores in all sources of ratings. The above analysis clearly shows that there is a definite relationship between scoring on Factor-Q_4 and the role performance of adult continuing education workers.

Conclusions

In brief, the results relating to the influence of personality factors on the role performance of adult continuing education workers suggests that the effective adult continuing education worker seems to posses the majority of traits exhibited by low scorers on Factor C, E, H, L, M, N, Q_2 and Q_3. On the otherhand, the qualities attributed to maximum scorers on Factor-A, B, F, I and Q4. Whereas, the traits attributed to top scorers on Factors Q, O and Q_2; are also appear to be desirable for good adult continuing education worker.

6

Summary and Conclusions

Introduction

Education plays a dominant role in the development of human resources in any country. Realizing this, the Government of India launched National Adult Education Programme on October 2, 1978 to eradicate illiteracy in the age group between 15 and 35 years. Later, the programmes are further strengthened by launching National Literacy Mission to cover 80 million illiterates in the country by 1995. In the NLM provision is made for providing literacy, post-literacy and continuing education activities.

The success of the programme largely depends upon the performance of the adult continuing education workers. As a grassroot level worker and actual does of the adult education programme at the community level, he/she has to play a diversified roles to make the programme a success. The ability to play his roles successfully presupposes utmost efficiency on the part of the adult continuing education workers. The performance of the adult continuing education worker depends upon his personal characteristics, his personality traits and his attitude towards adult education programme. The present study has been undertaken with the following objectives.

Objectives

(i) To device the instrument to measure the role performance of adult continuing education workers.

(ii) To study the influence of sex, age, educational qualification and community background on the role performance of adult continuing education workers.

(iii) To study the influence of sex, age, educational qualification and community background of the adult continuing education workers and their attitude towards adult education.

(iv) To know the place of adult continuing education workers attitude towards adult education on his role performance.

(v) To examine how the personality characteristics are related to the role performance of adult continuing education workers.

Hypotheses

Based on the above objectives, the following hypotheses were formulated for testing.

(i) There exists significant difference in the role performance of audlt continuing education workers due to variation in their sex.

(ii) There exists significant difference the role performance of the adult continuing education workers due to variation in their age.

(iii) There exists significant difference in the role performance of adult continuing education workers due to variation in their community.

(v) There is significant difference in the attitude of adult continuing education workers towards adult education due to variation in their sex.

(vi) There is significant difference in the attitude of adult continuing education workers towards adult education due variation in their age, educational qualifications and community background.

(vii) There is significant difference between adult continuing education workers representing difference levels of positive attitude and their role performance.

(viii) There is significant difference between adult continuing education workers representing different levels of scoring on each one of the 16 Personality Factors (as Measured by Cattle's 16 P.F.) and their role performance as adult continuing education workers.

Need and Importance of the Study

Illiteracy is one of the major problems of our country. To boost literacy and post-literacy programmes, the Government of India, started National Literacy Mission on May, 1988. For promoting post literacy and continuing education for neo-literates and school dropouts, a good number of post-literacy and continuing educational workers have been appointed. The post-literacy or continuing education worker is not limited to instruction. At the same time, he also expects to play a predominent role to activate the community to take up developmental tasks in that community. In other words, we may say, for proper functioning o the continuing education centre the instructor has to play three major roles i.e., teaching roles, organising roles and community roles. The efficiency or performance of the continuing education worker to a large extent depends on how effectively he/she discharges the role expected of him/her.

In the performance of the above stated roles, several factors may come into the way of continuing education workers such as age, sex, educational qualification and community, personality, and attitude of the adult continuing education workers.

Methodology

For the purpose of the study, the following are the tools developed by the investigator.

1. The adult continuing education workers Role Performance Scale is developed by the investigator. The scale consisted of 36 items comprising teaching activities, organisational activities and community related activities. The items can be rated on 5 response categories.
2. The adult continuing education workers attitude towards adult education programme is measured by administering a 5 point attitude scale developed by the investigator. The scale consisted on 30 statements both positive and negative indicators. The scores of an instructor on the scale will range between 30 and 150.
3. Cattle's 16 Personality Factors Form-E is adopted for the purpose of the present study to measure the personality factors and characteristics of adult continuing education workers.

Apart from the above, the personal information related to the adult continuing education workers such as sex, age, educational qualification and community background are collected.

Sample

For the purpose of the study, the investigator requires three types of respondents namely—Adult continuing education workers, community leaders and neo-literates. As a part of National Literacy Mission, total literacy and post literacy programmes are in operation in various districts of Tamil Nadu. In the first stage, the investigator selected 2 post-literacy districts (Madurai and Tanjore Districts) by using simple random sampling technique from among the various post-literacy districts of Tamil Nadu. In both these districts, post literacy programmes are in operation at the time of conducting this investigation. At the second stage, the investigator selected 50 Adult continuing education workers from each post literacy districts by using stratified random sampling technique considering their sex, age, educational status and community background, as stratas. In the third stage, two neo-literates under each adult continuing education worker will be selected thus totalling 200 neo-literates of the study. Thus the total sample consists of 100 adult continuing education workers, 200 neo-literates and 100 community leaders.

Data Collection and Analysis

The required data is collected from the selected sample by administering the following tools to the following sample.

(i) The role performance scale is administered to the adult continuing education workers to get self rating.

(ii) Community representatives to get community ratings.

(iii) Neo-literates for neo-literate ratings.

(iv) The ratings of above three groups form cumulative ratings.

(v) A five point attitude scale is administered on adult continuing education workers to know their attitude towards the various aspects of adult education programme.

(vi) Cattle's–16 P.F. Form-E is administered to adult continuing education workers to get their score on 16 P.F. Similarly, the personal information such as sex, age, educational background and community of the adult continuing education workers is collected from them.

The data obtained is analysed by using mean, standard deviation, t-test and F-ratio.

Major Findings and Conclusions

(i) Sex of the adult/continuing education workers significantly influenced their role performance as per community ratings. Women are rated as better role performers than men adult continuing education workers. On the other hand, sex has not influenced the role performance of adult continuing education workers as per self, neo-literate and cumulative ratings.

(ii) Age of the adult continuing education workers significantly influenced in their role performance as per self ratings. The lower age group (i.e. 21–30) workers are rated as better role performance than the other two age groups. On the other hand, age has not influenced the role performance of adult/continuing education workers as per community, neo-literate and cumulative ratings.

(iii) Educational qualification of the adult continuing education workers significantly influenced their role performance as per community ratings, neo-literate ratings and cumulative ratings. The higher educational qualification workers perform better than the other groups.

(iv) Community of the adult/continuing education workers significantly influenced their role performance as per self, neo-literate and cumulative ratings. The backward community workers perform better than the other two communities. On the other hand, community is not a factor in influencing the role performance of adult/continuing education workers, as per community ratings.

(v) Sex has not significantly influenced the adult continuing education workers attitude towards adult education.

(vi) Similarly, age has not significantly influenced the attitude of adult continuing education workers towards adult education.

(vii) Level of attitude of the adult continuing education workers significantly influenced their role performance as per neo-literates ratings. The high (positive) attitude workers perform better than the low and medium attitude groups. On the other hand, the level of attitude has not influenced, the adult continuing education workers role performance as per self, community and cumulative ratings.

(viii) There is significant difference between the mean performance scores of adult continuing education workers representing low, medium, and top scores as per neo-literates ratings on Factor-A. Further, it is noted that adult continuing education workers scoring medium score on Factor-A proves to be the better performance in their roles than the low and top scores. On the otherhand, there is no significant differences between the mean performance scores of adult continuing education workers representing low, medium and top scores on Factor-A, as per the self-community and cumulative ratings.

(ix) There is significant difference between the mean performance scores of the adult continuing education workers representing low, medium and top scores on Factor-B as per neo-literate ratings only. Furhter, the adult continuing education workers scoring medium score on Factor-B proved to be better performance than the low and top scorers. On the otherhand, there is no significant differences between the adult continuing education workers representing low, medium and top scorers on Factor-B as per self, community and cumulative ratings.

(x) There is no significant difference between the mean performance scores of the adult continuing education workers representing low, medium, and top scoring groups on Factor-C as per self, community, neo-literate and cumulative ratings.

(xi) There is no significant difference between the mean performance scores of the adult continuing education workers representing low, medium and top scoring groups on Factor-E as per all ratings (self, community, neo-literate and cumulative ratings).

(xii) Ther is no significant difference between the mean performance scores of the adult continuing education workers representing low, medium and top scoring groups on Factor-E as per all ratings (self, community, neo-literate and cumulative ratings).

(xiii) There is significant difference between the mean performance scores of the adult continuing education workers representing low, medium and top scoring groups on Factor-G as per community ratings only. Further, the adult continuing education workers scoring top scores on Factor-G proved to be better performers than the low and medium scorers. On the other hand, there is no significant differences between the mean performance scores of adult continuing education workers representing low, medium and top scorers on Factor-G as per self, neo-literate and cumulative ratings.

(xiv) There is no significant difference between the mean performance scores of the adult continuing education workers representing low, medium and top scoring groups on Factor-H as per all ratings (self, community and literate and cumulative ratings).

(xv) There is no significant difference between the mean performance scores of the adult continuing education workers representing the low, medium and top scoring groups on Factor-I as per all ratings (self, community, neo-literate and cumulative ratings).

(xvi) There is significant difference between the mean performance scores of adult continuing education workers representing low, medium and top scorers on Factor-L as per self, neo-literates and cumulative ratings. Further, it is noted that adult continuing education workers scoring low on Factor-L, proved to be better performance than the medium and top scorers. On the other hand, there is a significant difference between the mean performance scores of adult continuing education workers representing low, medium and to scoring groups on Factor-L, as per community ratings.

(xvii) There is no significant difference between the mean performance scores of the adult continuing education workers representing low, medium and top scorers on Factor-M as per all ratings i.e., self, community, neo-literate and cumulative ratings.

(xviii) There is significant difference between the mean performance scores of the adult continuing education workers representing low, medium and top scorers on Factor-N as per self, neo-literate and cumulative ratings. Further, it is noted that adult continuing education workers scoring medium scores proved to be better performers than the low and top scorers. On the other hand, there is no significant difference between the adult continuing education workers representing low, medium and top scores on Factor-N, as per community ratings.

(xix) There is no signficant difference between the mean performance scores of the adult continuing education workers representing low, medium and top scores on Factor-O as per all ratings (self, community, neo-literate and cumulative ratings).

(xx) There is no significant difference between the mean difference scores of the adult continuing education workers representing low, medium and top scorers on Factor-Q_1 as per all the ratings i.e., self, community, neo-literate and cumulative ratings.

(xxi) There is no significant difference between the mean performance scores of the adult continuing education workers representing low, medium and top scorers on Factor-Q_2 as per all rating i.e., self, community, neo-literate and cumulative ratings.

(xxii) There is significant difference between the mean performance scorers of the adult continuing education workers representing low, medium and top scorers on Factor-Q_3 as per neo-literate and cumulative ratings. Further, it is noted that the adult continuing education workers scoring low scores proved to be better performance than the medium and top scorers. On the other hand, there is not significant difference between the mean performance scores of adult continuing education representing low medium and top scorers on Factor-Q_3 as per self and community ratings.

(xxiii) There is significant difference between the mean performance scores of adult continuing education workers representing low, medium and top scorers on Factor-Q_4 as per self, neo-literate and cumulative ratings. Further, it is noted that the adult continuing education workers scoring medium scores, proved to be better performers than the low and top scorers. On the other hand, there is no significant difference between the mean performance scores of adult continuing education workers representing low, medium and top scorers on Factor-Q_4 as per community ratings.

Bibliography

Aker, G.F. (1962) : "A study of certain factors relatng to the instructors effectiveness in the Adult Education Programme". M.A. Dissertation, S.V. University.

Alkana and Heuriques (1982) : "Functioning of the Adult Education Programme in Maharashtra, Bombay : Tata Institute of Social Sciences.

Ankaiah (1982) : "A study of the instructors interest in participation in Adult Education Programme". M.A. dissertation, S.V. University.

Bhandari and Mehta 91974) : "Teacher Characteristics and Class Room Factors in relation to persistance and Dropout". *Australian Journal of Adult Education*, XIV (2), p. 60–64.

Bledsoe, J.C. and Brown, D. (1968) : "Role Perceptions of Secondary Teachers as related to Pupils Perceptions of Teacher Behavioural Characteristics". *The Journal of Educational Research*, Vol. 61, No. 9, pp. 422–29.

Cattell, R.B. (1965) : "16 PF Questionnaire : Manual Supplement for Form-E". *Illinois* : The Institute for Personality and Ability Testing.

Cass, A.W. (1971) : "Materials and Methods for Adult Literacy Programmes". *Literacy Discussion*, II(3), 22–23.

Chamberline, M.N. (1960) : "The Competencies of Adult Educators". *Adult Education*, II, 78–83.

ChatterJee and Others (1969) : "Voluntary Action for Adult Literacy: A Report of Gramdan Shikshan Yajna at Darbhanga and Mirjopur". Varanasi : Navachetna PrakashaN, 128.

Cobley, L.S. (1976) : "The Qualities Required of Teachers of Agriculture". Training of Agriculture and Rural Development, Paris, UNESCO, 54–59.

Grabowski, S.M. (1976) : "Training Teachers of Adult : Models and Innovative Programmes". Occasional, Paper No. : 46, Syracuse University.

Hariharan, R. and Rao, T.V. (1982) : "Adult Education in Rajasthan—Third appraisal (Jhunjhunu district)". Ahmedabad : Indian Institute of Management.

Janardhana Naidu, G. (1980) : "A study of the Farmers Attitude Towards the National Adult Education Programme in Sri Kalahasthi Project". M.A. Dissertation, S.V. University.

Krishna Reddy (1981) : "A Study of the Job Satisfaction of NAEP Instructors". M.A. dissertation, S.V. University.

Knox, A.B. (1971) : "Inservice Education in Adult Basic Education". Tallahasses : Florida Sate-University.

Madana Mohan Reddy (1985) : "Performance requirements of Adult Education Instructors as perceived by the Instructors of Adult Education Centres". M.A. dissertation, S.V. University.

Mandry, A.C. (1963) : "The Functions and Training Needs of Adult Education Directors in Public School Systems". Ohio : Ohio State University.

Malakondaiah, C.C. (1980) : "Characteristics of an effective instructor". M.A. Dissertation, S.V. University.

Mathur, A.K. (1975) : "Some Characteristics of a Teacher as liked by Illiterate Adults". Indian Journal of Adult Education, 36(10), 14–15.

Mocker, D.W. (1974) : "The Identification, Classification and Ranking of Knowledge, Behaviours and Attitudes Appropriate for Adult Basic Education Teachers" Ed. D. Dissertation, State University of New York at Albany.

Mourad, F. (1971) : "Literacy teachers in the Algerian Functional Literacy Project". Literacy Discussion, II(2), 149–157.

Munuswamy, N. (1980) : "The Attitude of Adult Education Instructors towards the NAEP in Sri Kalahasthi Block". M.A. dissertation, S.V. University.

Muthuchamy, I. (1991) : "Role-performance of Adult Continuing Education prevails working in Rural Functional Literacy Projects of Tamil Nadu State". M.Phil dissertaion, Alagappa University, Karaikudi.

Nath, J.C. (1981) : "Attitude of NSS Adult Education Organisers towards NAEP". M.A. dissertation, S.V. University.

Pandiyammal, K. (1989) : "Competencies needed for Adult Education Animators". M.Phil. dissertation, GRU, Gandhigram.

Pearce (1960) : "Basic Education Teachers : Seven Needed Qualities". U.S. Department of Health, Education and Welfare.

Reddy, P.A. and Kumaraswamy, T. (1984) : "Qualities of an Effective Adult Education Organiser from Supervisors Point of View". Experiments in Education, XII (1), 10–14.

Reddy, P.A. and Reddy, G.C. (1985) : "Characteristics of an Effective Instructor : A Study". Indian Journal of Adult Education, 46(2), 27–29.

Reddy, P.A. (1985) : "An Investigation into the Relationship between Instructor Effectiveness and Some Selected Variables". Prasac, 11 (3- & 4-), 8–13.

Reddy, P.A. (1989) : "A Study of Certain Psychological Factors relating to Adult Education Instructor Effectiveness". Doctoral thesis S.V. University.

Reddy, G.L. (1985) : "Discrepancy between Ideology and Practice of Instructor roles as perceived by National Adult Education Programme Instructors". M.Phil dissertation, S.V. University.

Reddy, P.A. (1992) : "Determinants of Adult Education Instructor Effectiveness". Uppal Publishing House, New Delhi.

Report of the Work Oriented Adult Literacy Project, Iran (1973) : "Final Technical Report in Literacy Teachers : Interpretative Bibliography". Tehran : IIALM, 1978.

Reddeppa, G. (1993) : "The Study of determinants of Prerak Effectiveness". M.Phil dissertation, S.V. University.

Rogers, W. Oxford (1969) : "Adult Education : The Open Door". Pensylvania : International Text Book Co.

Soles, S. (1964) : "Teacher Role Expectations and the Internal Organisation of Secondary Schools". Journal of Educational Research L III, pp. 227–238.

Sorenson, Husex and Constance Yu. (1963) : "Divergent Excepts of teacher role : An approach to the measurement of teacher effectiveness". Journal of Educational Psychology, LIV, pp. 287–94.

Srivastava, (1981) : "Literacy Work among Small Farmers and Tribes". Marwah Publications, New Delhi.

Subhashini (1985) : "Communication Barriers in Teaching Adults as Perceived by Adult Education Instructors". M.A. dissertation, S.V. University.

Tripathi, V. (1977) : "Training of Instructors for Non-formal Education Programme". Literacy work, 6(2), 35–50.

Veri, C.C. (1968) : "The Design of Doctoral Programme in Adult Education based on the expressed needs of Professional Practitioners". Doctoral Thesis, University of Nebraska.

Vijayalakshmi, A. (1985) : "Opinion of Adult Education Instructors about their Profession and Adult Education in General". M.A. dissertation, S.V. University.

White, T.J. (1950) : "Similarity of Training Interest among Adult Education Leaders". Ph.D. Thesis, University of chicago.

Yasanna (1986) : "A Study of Certain Factors relating to the Instructors Effectiveness in the Adult Education Programme". M.A. dissertation, S.V. University.

Index